TAIL

text and pictures

Deepa Balsavar

Tulika

Tail (English)
ISBN 978-81-8146-576-4

First published in India 2009
Reprinted in 2015

Published by
Tulika Publishers, 24/1 Ganapathy Colony Third Street, Teynampet, Chennai 600 018, India
email tulikabooks@vsnl.com *website* www.tulikabooks.com

Printed and bound by
Sudarsan Graphics, 27 Neelkanta Mehta Street, T. Nagar, Chennai 600 017, India

If Thumb Thumb Thambi had a tail...

He would wag it to show he is happy.

He would swish it to keep flies away.

He would swing from
tree to tree.

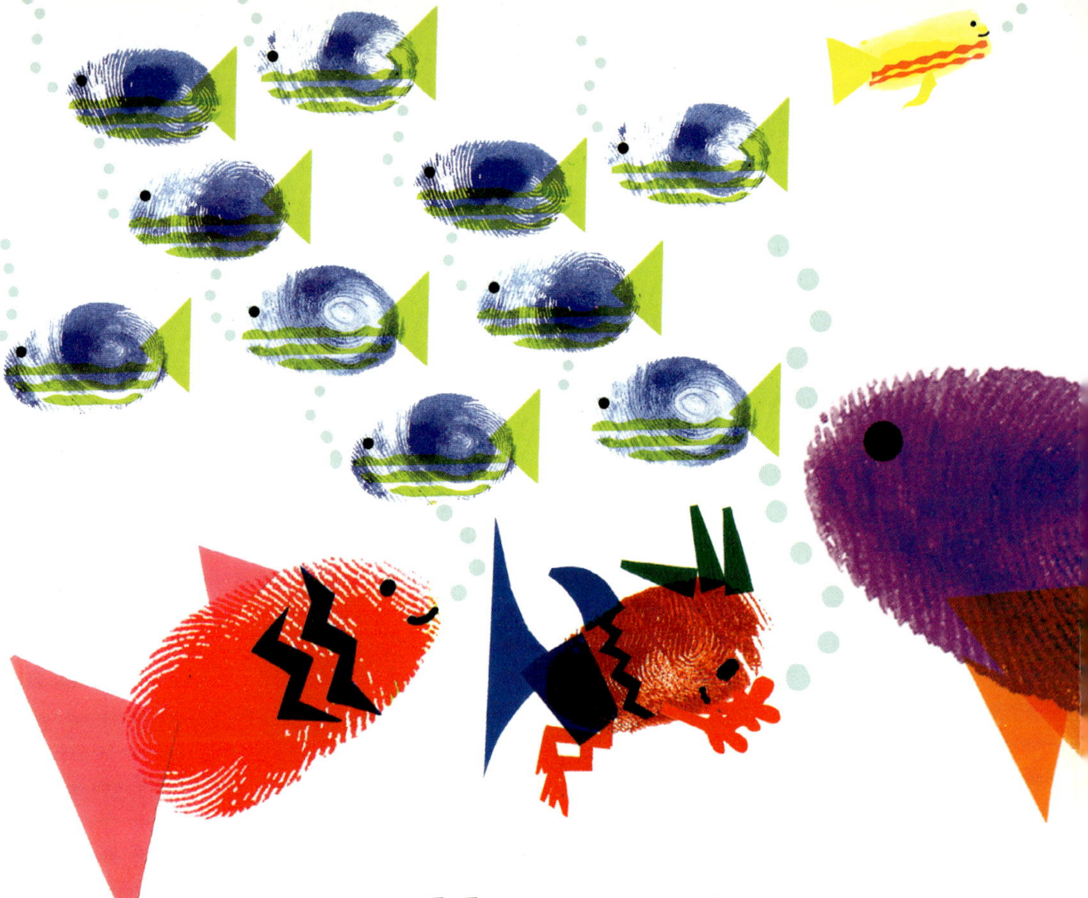

He would even swim

to the bottom of the sea.

If Thumb Thumb Thambi had a tail

surely he would fly!

The story is over. Let's draw.

This is Thumb Thumb Thambi's favourite animal.

Put your thumbprint on this page and draw a picture.

This is my favourite animal.

I CAN READ THIS BOOK!